INTENTIONAL

SUCCESS

by:

Jenny Sevil

Intentional Success: Proven Mind Techniques To Improve Your Golf Game, From A 9 Time Tournament Winner

© 2017 Jenny Sevil

ISBN-13: 978-1977921727
ISBN-10:1977921728

Dedicated to:

Warren ...... Forever my support and number one fan.

My parents, extended family and the many friends who supported me through the ups and downs.

Ryan and Laura for making me understand true success.......

DOWNLOAD YOUR FREE BONUSES AT

jennysevilthemindgame.com.au/bonuses

Table of Contents

Foreword

I first met Jen in 1987 in France. She was there with husband Warren in a clapped out camper van. We struck up a friendship right away and in those early days it looked like Jen might struggle a bit.

Over the next few years she proved us all wrong and with an incredible strong mind and a much stronger game she soon started playing some very solid golf.

Then she took a very brave decision to go to Japan to play on the JLPGA tour with no knowledge of the language and culture.

This is where Jenny really thrived but without that switched on mind and clear thought process, in my opinion, she would never have gone on to be such a good tour pro racking up many wins.

- Dame Laura Davies

(World Golf Hall of Fame; Friend)

A "For as it's a team effort—we've done it all together," says Jenny, with husband Warren. "He's quite famous in Japan as well."

THE ANONYMOUS SUPERSTAR

Golfer Jenny Sevil has won titles galore, but fame eludes her here at home

WHEN GOLFER JENNY SEVIL returned home from a tour of Japan last December, the local Gold Coast Ford Australia dealership lent her a brand new jet-black Capri with her name emblazoned on both sides. Sevil had already cashed in three cars won in the space of a year, but she didn't refuse this customised set of wheels. The reaction the car provoked from other drivers was a little hard to take, though. "I'd pull up at a traffic light and people would look over and go, 'Who's Jenny Sevil?'" she says with a laugh. "My next goal is to become a Trivial Pursuit question."

These days it's easy for Sevil, 29, to laugh off such ignorance—her success

1992, she finished the year ranked 15th on the Japanese tour. In golf-crazed Japan, Sevil, the only non-Asian in the Top 50, can hardly make it from one street corner to the next without being recognised. In Australia she is one of the highest-paid female athletes and was Australia's top female golfer of 1992—but no-one knows her.

Anonymous or not, Sevil and her husband, Warren, 30, who doubles as her caddy and coach, are clearly enjoying their good fortune. "Have you ever seen a bedroom this big?" asks Jenny, giving a tour of their three-bedroom Gold Coast flat. Indeed, the top-floor master suite runs the length of the unit and has two verandas overlooking Currumbin Beach.

tournament when Jenny was 15. For Warren, it was love at first sight. "I couldn't imagine my life continuing without being married to her," he says. Jenny had other ideas. She had followed parents Allan Jones, a small-business manager, and Rita, a housewife, around the local course from the age of 7. "To think that I was good enough to be a professional was a lot of a dream," says Jenny. "But you've got to have those dreams to keep you going." She accepted a golf scholarship at Mississippi State University in 1982 and left Warren behind.

When Sevil returned to Queensland two years later, Warren suggested she move to Sydney, where he worked for QTC and played at the Bonnie Doon Golf Club. "Warren and Dad were

My Story

I am Jenny Sevil. I have been a professional golfer for thirty years and played full time on Tour for seven of those years.

I was a reasonably good amateur golfer, a scratch handicapper. I represented my state of New South Wales and was also the first Australian female golfer to receive a golf scholarship to a US College (Mississippi State University.)

I was no Karrie Webb, Lydia Ko or Tiger Woods (whom everyone knew would win soon after turning professional). Instead, when I turned professional, I would probably have been voted by my peers as the one LEAST likely to succeed.

At the time when I decided to make the transition from amateur to professional golf, many people doubted I would make a career of it. I heard on the golfing grapevine that "I would never make a cent from the game." So, off to the Ladies European Tour I went, and

..... proved all those doubters RIGHT!

I missed cut after cut by one shot, made very little prize money and my self-esteem was at an all time low.

I returned home, broke, disheartened and convinced I had made the wrong decision. I wondered if I should "get a real job."

My husband (Warren) and I were living in Sydney at the time and I went back to waitressing, cleaning houses and bar tending to help pay the bills.

I was on my way to one of those jobs one morning when I heard an advertisement on the radio for an upcoming personal development course. It wasn't a sports related course, but it caught my attention.

There was very little awareness of sports psychology in those days so that avenue was foreign and not an option for me. I was, however, desperate and knew that if I was to continue with my golf, I had to try something different! I signed up for the course with the support of my husband (Warren) and his credit card.

We had just one hundred dollars in the bank yet decided we would borrow and both attend the course with a view to this being a "life-changer.

THE PERSONAL DEVELOPMENT COURSE WENT FOR THREE DAYS, AND FROM IT I ABSORBED AN ABUNDANCE OF INFORMATION THAT I ADAPTED TO MY GOLF GAME.

THIS WAS THE MOMENT THAT CHANGED MY LIFE AND CAREER DRAMATICALLY.

Returning to tournament competition, I went on to win nine professional events in Australia and Japan and became the number one ranked female player in Australia the following year. I earned more than three million dollars over the next six years.

When I first started my "mind game" business, I felt uncomfortable about telling people of my achievements and certainly did not want to mention how much money I made from golf. To me that was very un-Australian. I now embrace my achievements and find it necessary to mention my earnings and victories as testimony in convincing others that what I teach and share, really does work.

Ready to give the game away, unable to make cuts, to winning tournaments and becoming number one!

Being Told You're Not Good Enough

The story I am about to share with you, is one which I hope will inspire you to hold on to your dreams, no matter how big or small they are.

When I first earned my playing card to compete on the Japan Ladies Professional Golf Tour, I was 'over the moon,' bursting with excitement and couldn't wait to get started. My excitement was short lived, however, when I realised I didn't have the money to pay the joining fee of AUD$6,000, nor the $1,500 weekly expenses to be "on Tour."

After seeing my distress and understanding my predicament, a Japanese friend took me to meet with one of the biggest sporting companies in Japan. He was confident they would be able to assist me or offer some advice as to how I could find some form of financial support. When I arrived at their office, I was told they couldn't help me. They were very blunt in explaining that it would be difficult for me to attract sponsorship because, firstly, I was too old (at 26!); secondly, I had no record of success;

Furthermore, I was married and in their eyes, not marketable.

Can you imagine how I felt after I left that meeting in Osaka? I was more than deflated. I wanted to crawl into a hole. It was difficult for me to see a clear path, to maintain the belief that I could still achieve my dream.

When I returned to Australia after the meeting, I was more determined than ever to succeed and to show everyone I could do it! I continued to work hard on my golf game and my mental strength, practicing both, every moment of every day.

I told myself to remember that when one door closes, another one opens. As my Japanese Father (Max, who adopted me as part of his Japanese family) told me, "you need to fight!" So, I did.

Max was a very wealthy Japanese businessman who sponsored me through the six months of the Japan qualifying school. Once I got through this tough stage, I expected Max would continue with his financial and moral support. He didn't. He told me it would not be good business for him to sponsor me because he wanted Warren and I to be part of his family, and he didn't want to risk that relationship through business ties. I was devastated but understood this was the Japanese way and that I WOULD need to fight, be hungry and earn success through determination and dedication.

Things did turn around for me. Twelve months later I won a major tournament in Japan as well as a high profile tournament in Australia. I had secured a high paying sponsorship deal in Japan, and was ranked among the top fifteen players in Japan, and number one on the Australian Tour.

Have you ever been told you are not good enough? Have you ever been knocked down, told you are too old, too young, too fat, not right for the position???

I want you to be armed with the tools, the techniques and the confidence to get back up, to believe in yourself, and show those knockers that you are not taking their negativity on board. Their comments and statements are NOT your truth!

Stand Guard
at the Door
of Your Mind

-Jim Rohn

Intentional Success

Your dreams may not include winning golf tournaments, but you will come across people in your life who will, or who have already, tried to knock the wind out of your sails, suggesting no hope for you achieving your goals.

Family and friends often suggest a "secure option" or a "real job" instead of supporting your ambition to follow your dreams.

In the early days of my golfing career I could have accepted the secure option and given up on my dream, but I chose to ignore the doubters and back myself. I took the following approach to deal with those negative comments.

> ➢ **I decided I had a choice**. We all do. If you have a dream or a goal, you can choose to go after it. You can choose to go after it or believe what others say and take on their negativity. If you choose the latter, your dreams are then lost. I chose not to let the words - "you'll never make a cent from the game" - "unlikely to succeed" - "too old" - "unmarketable" deflate my dream or damage my self-esteem (well not for too long anyway.) It was difficult hearing those comments, and I was hurt. My response, however, was to use this as fuel to drive me harder and make me more determined to succeed and prove them wrong.

➢ **Stay focused on your intentions/purpose and what you want to achieve.** Know that focus and action equals results. I never let go of my dream of being a successful golfer, even though there were tough times and people who believed I wouldn't make it.

➢ **Never allow others to take your power.** Other people's words can be damaging if we allow them to be. Choose to not allow others to take away your power whether it relates to your career, your relationships or your own personal goals. Stay determined and true to yourself.

I believe each one of us deserves to follow our dreams. Should you be prepared to help yourself by understanding you always have a choice to focus on what you want, and to hold on to your personal power, you will have the ability to create the life and the success you deserve.

Remember, life is what YOU, no-one else, decide to make it!

Make it Your Choice to "Intentionally" Create Your Own "Success"!

Revealing My Mind Game Techniques

Here are some of the techniques / tools I developed, to help create my own success.

1. **Catch Your Thinking**

   This relates to awareness of the thoughts you have running through your head. Learn to listen to what you are saying to yourself on the way to golf, before you play a shot and even after you have played a shot. Think about it – have you ever caught yourself thinking or telling yourself any of the following:

   - **"I knew I shouldn't have come to golf today"**
   - **"I always play this hole badly"**
   - **After one bad shot, "Oh it's going to be one of those days"**
   - **"I can't hit out of bunkers"**
   - **"I hate using my 5 iron"**
   - **"My putting is hopeless at the moment"**
   - **"Oh no, not the water hole!"**

These are just a few examples of how we sabotage or self-destruct, purely because of our mind's thoughts and the way we talk to ourselves.

2. Delete Negative Thoughts

Once you have learned to recognise (the awareness) damaging or negative thoughts, you must STOP, acknowledge that you are having a negative thought, tell yourself that you are going to delete that thought and give it no power!

Next, you replace the negative thought with a positive statement relating to the preferred outcome of your shot.

This is how we deal with the negative chatter in our heads:

Re: "I knew I shouldn't have come to golf today."

Recognise, delete then insert:

"Today is going to be a great day, I will play well and enjoy the game."

Re: "I always play this hole badly."

Recognise, delete then insert:

"It is just another hole; I can master it by focusing on my routine on each shot."

Re: After one bad shot, "Oh it's going to be one of those days."

Recognise, delete then insert:

"Even the best players hit poor shots, I am not going to let one bad shot ruin my day."

Re: "I can't hit out of bunkers"
Recognise, delete then insert:

"The bunker is my friend; I am a great bunker player."

What Are You Feeding Your Mind?

Re: "I hate using my 5 iron"
Recognise, delete then insert:

"I am going to swing this club just as I do my favourite pitching wedge"

Re: "My putting is hopeless at the moment."
Recognise, delete then insert:

"From this point onwards, I decide my putting will improve. I am a great putter."

Re: "Oh no, not the water hole!"
Recognise, delete then insert:

"What water? The water is not my target; I will hit my target!"

*The Mind Does Not Judge
What You Tell It ...*

*THE MIND <u>BELIEVES </u>WHAT
YOU TELL IT!*

*Therefore, feed it positive
productive information.*

Routine & Repetition Creates Good Habits

3.   The Importance of a Pre-shot-Routine

A pre-shot routine involves the process you go through from the time it is your turn to play, to the time you make your first movement to execute a shot. The routine can involve one or more actions, habits, idiosyncrasies including: standing behind the ball and visualizing the shot; taking one practice swing; taking two practice swings; placing the club behind the ball then taking your stance; a couple of waggles of the club whilst you again visualize the shot; a forward press as the last movement before you commence your backswing.

We all have different "habits," different movements that we have developed, to prepare us for the execution of the golf shot. Some players simply walk up to the ball, place the club behind the ball, take their stance, take one look at the target, then execute. Others have a more deliberate and multi-faceted routine. We are all different. The key, however, is to have a pre-shot routine which is the same every time, with every club. A pre-shot routine must be simple and repetitive. This is crucial!

A repetitive pre-shot routine creates one set of thoughts which the mind will reproduce, allowing no scope for negative or multiple thoughts as you prepare to execute a shot.

Replicating the routine on your tee shot, fairway woods, irons, chipping and putting, leaves no margin for distractions which could sabotage the execution of the shot.

The mind is busy processing positive swing thoughts and focusing ONLY on the execution of the shot at hand.

A pre-shot routine can also relieve nerves.

Frequent rehearsal results in improved performance and consistency

4. Pick a Target

If I were playing darts, I wouldn't just throw the dart at the wall in the hope of hitting somewhere on the board. I would focus on the dartboard itself, and then zoom in on the Bullseye as my specific target. If I were to miss the bullseye, I am confident I would still have hit somewhere within the outer ring.

Similarly, if I stand on the teeing ground and look forward and "just try it and hit it down there somewhere," the ball will finish somewhere/ anywhere, but not necessarily on the fairway.

Therefore, I must decide on a specific target such as the middle of the fairway, a sprinkler on the left side of the fairway or that brown patch on the right hand side. Even if my ball doesn't land on that exact target, it is likely to be in the vicinity and still in play. Pick a small target, zoom in on a bullseye spot on the fairway, narrow it down.

On every shot, be precise about your target. Think of it as you would when zooming in with a camera lens OR as you would when you crop a photograph. In either process, you are eliminating areas that are not part of your focus.

Often when golfers stand on the tee, they focus on the trees in the rough, the fairway bunkers, the out-of-bounds or the fact that there is a water carry.

You Can't Hit a Target If You Don't Have One

If the mind is thinking trees, bunker, water, OB, that thought becomes its focus. It is therefore CRITICAL that you choose a small target so that your mind has one focal point only.

Focus on What You Want More Of

5. Focus on the Good Shots

Are you guilty of the following?

You have finished your round. You played OK, maybe not your best but it was a round made up of some good shots and some bad. You walk into the clubhouse and someone asks "How did you play?"

You immediately respond with "Oh well if it wasn't for the triple bogey on the 5th, or the out of bounds on the 7th or the 3-putt on the last hole, I would have had a good round."

WHY IS IT THAT SO MANY GOLFERS FOCUS THEIR POST ROUND REVIEW ON THE ONE BAD SHOT OR THE ONE BAD HOLE?

Why are we reluctant to say that we played well, that we hit a great drive on the 4th hole, that we sank a 30-foot putt to save par on the 17th or that we holed a bunker shot?

We seem to be more comfortable re-living the bad shots.

Perhaps we are uncomfortable recalling the good shots because other players might think we are "big-noting" or big-headed or arrogant.

As most of us are uncomfortable sharing our good shots, and if you catch yourself doing the same, this is what I suggest you do;

Ask yourself ......

What was

My best

Shot Today?

After golf, perhaps when driving home, ask yourself, "What was my best shot today?" "What did I do that was good out there today?"

Re-live the good shots and inwardly celebrate. Doing this will make you feel better about your golf so that when you next tee it up, you will have a positive recollection of your last game.

Reminding yourself of your good shots will build confidence and help you focus on positives rather than negatives. Your mind will remember the visuals of the good shots that you have chosen to make your focus.

Understanding Negative Thinking

There has been much written and taught about the power of positive thinking. I for one have long embraced this notion, the awareness of our feelings, and the ability to create outcomes in our lives as a result of a positive attitude and mind control.

My philosophy of creating "intentional success" is based around the positive. It is, however, impossible to eliminate or fight negative thinking and negative outcomes during a round of golf, or throughout life in general.

Trying to maintain an all or nothing "positive attitude" can be dangerous. It is SO important that we recognise and accept this fact otherwise we will create pressure and stress in setting unrealistic goals.

Negative thinking will never go away, HOWEVER, the power lies in what you do with that thought.

You can't control your first (negative) thought, but the following thought you CAN control.

The Power Of Acceptance Of The Negative

How do we find a balance between positive and negative thinking? The power comes from the AWARENESS!

You may not recognise negative thinking in your life or in your golf game, you may just accept that "things aren't working for you" or that "that's the way things are in life." There are however, certain negative thought patterns. See if you identify with any of the following expressions:

All-or-nothing thinking: "I have to do things perfectly, and anything less than perfect is a failure" E.g. On the golf course, expecting the perfect shot **every** time.

Focusing on the negatives: Nothing ever goes my way – it is just one disappointment after another. E.g. You can't handle a bad bounce, or a bad lie. (Learn to accept that everyone gets bad bounces, the ground has imperfections!)

<u>Negative self-labelling</u>: "I'm a failure." "I am useless" Do you curse and abuse yourself after a bad shot?

<u>Catastrophism</u>: "My putts always lip-out!"

The power of acceptance of the above examples lies in the way you handle these situations. The way to improve has more to do with how you react to your bad shots (your "C Game") rather than expecting perfection and trying to improve on your "A Game."

Understanding that golf is NOT a game played perfectly, that there is rarely a perfect shot or a perfect round, will allow you to accept and handle the negative ie. the not-so-good shot, or not-so-good-round.

Note: Most people would rate a hole-in-one as the "perfect shot" but there are many aces that are a result of a mis-hit, lucky bounce, ball running along the ground or bouncing off a tree etc. Is there such a thing as the perfect shot anyway? We all play at different levels and we therefore have varying expectations.

Anger

Doubt

Frustration

I must be perfect!

Give up

Emotions Affect Performance

Let's try to understand the consequences of negative thoughts and self-doubt.

1. Fear: "I hope I don't play badly today"

2. Doubt: "I can't hit over that water. I can never play the 12th hole"

3. Anger: "Screw this! I give up. I am useless. I don't know why I bother coming to golf."

4. Frustration: "It's no use." "I hit it great on the practice range yet am hopeless on the golf course"

5. High Expectations: "I must hit every shot long and straight." "I must not miss any putts under six feet."

The POWER is in the NOW

Now, think about the above emotions and declarations. Are these serviceable reactions, manageable thoughts or mindsets? What do these have in common? They are judgements, which are a reaction to a focus on the RESULT.

Examples of results-based goals or expectations are:

- ✓ Trying to par a hole

- ✓ Trying to break your handicap

- ✓ Trying to win a competition

- ✓ Trying to get to No. 1

- ✓ Proving to someone that you are good or better than someone else.

We must change our thinking to create thoughts and assertions that focus on the NOW. To do this, we must direct our thinking around the PROCESS and the positive pathway to achieving the results.

The outcome is a result of the process!

So, What Is The Process??

The process is repeating what you do to create a good shot. That is, a simple swing thought, a simple repetitive ROUTINE! For me, whether I was playing my best or having a tough day, I always maintained one simple positive thought, and that was Turn – Wait – Drive! Turn – Wait – Drive! (Turn my shoulders, pause at top of swing and start my downswing with my leg drive)

It is so important to be aware of how we react to good and poor shots, as we accept the negative and focus on the positive.

<u>After a good shot</u>; watch it longer, stare it down and focus on it. Visualise that shot, replay the shot in your mind and store it in your memory. Remember there is a reason why you hit good shots ie. ROUTINE! Good posture, good fundamentals, good execution, positive thoughts. Remember this shot!

<u>After a poor shot</u>: Forget it. Dismiss it. Don't over-analyse! Switch off once you have seen where the ball finishes; instantly revert to that swing, that execution of the good shot you have stored in your mind; remember to focus on

ROUTINE and nothing else. Put all your energy into what went into the good shots.

"Keep it Simple"

Turn

Wait

Drive

A technical or swing coach will say you must understand the technical or fundamental cause of the bad shot. This can be true, however, to create more good shots you have to be able to recall and repeat the things you did <u>well</u>.

Don't focus on the things you did badly! It is important to understand your faults and most people will know their recurring fault. Never try something that is not part of your normal routine or swing process. Eg. "I might invent swing number 41(c) today!"

Golf – One shot at a time.

Life – One day at a time.

Business – One step at a time.

Let's Relate Golf to Life

GOLF'S "MIND GAME" TECHNIQUES PARALLEL WITH OUR APPROACH TO BUSINESS AND TO LIFE.

➢ Intentional Life

➢ Intentional Thinking

➢ Intentional Focus

➢ Intentional Desire

➢ Intentional Self Talk

Everything I apply to my golf game applies to my mental approach to business and my life.

The Power of Intentional thought

My old negative beliefs;

- ➤ I am a bad golfer, I should give up
- ➤ No one thinks I am any good
- ➤ I am always playing badly
- ➤ I struggle to make the cut
- ➤ Nobody likes me
- ➤ I am not as good as everyone else

What I Created through Intentional positive AFFIRMATIONS!

- ➤ I Jenny Sevil am a successful golfer
- ➤ I Jenny Sevil win tournaments
- ➤ I Jenny Sevil break course records
- ➤ I Jenny Sevil deserve the best in life
- ➤ I Jenny Sevil feel good about myself

Affirmations are powerful Mind Game tools. Affirmations are statements, declarations that you say to yourself, over and over.

Writing them down repeatedly is also very powerful!

You are affirming to yourself whatever it is you want to happen, or what you want to become your new reality!

What do you want to see in the mirror?

I am ....

.... a winner ....

.... successful ....

.... happy ....

What is Your Affirmation Statement?

I

AM

. . . .

Self Criticisms Re Golf

1. "I knew I shouldn't have come to golf today"

2. "I always play this hole badly"

3. After one bad shot, "Oh it's going to be one of those days"

4. "I can't hit out of bunkers"

5. "I hate using my 5 iron"

6. "My putting is hopeless at the moment"

7. "Oh no, not the water hole!"

Trust

Self Criticisms Re Business

1. After one bad phone call with client – "Oh it is going to be one of those days."

2. "Nothing is going right for me at work right now."

3. "This is a tough deal / contract, I don't know if I can get it done."

4. "Am I ever going to get a sale across the line? What am I doing wrong?"

5. "I always perform badly at interviews. I'll never get the job I want."

6. "I get so nervous speaking in front of my peers, I hope they don't criticise me."

7. "My motivation level is so low at the moment – no one believes in me."

Your Thoughts Create Your Reality

Self Criticisms Re Life

1. You wake up, it's raining, and you say "What an awful day."

2. Someone pulls out in front of you in traffic, you say "Great, one of those days" – (manifesting anger)

3. "I'm in a bad job, bad relationship and have an unhealthy lifestyle. I hate my life!"

4. "I really want to try something new, but I don't want people to judge me."

5. "My self-esteem is so low because I am useless at everything."

6. "Thinking of taking on a new challenge but will take the easy way out and stay in my comfort zone." (Minimising risk, afraid of the consequences of success).

7. Lack confidence in appearance; "I don't want to go out because everyone looks better than me."

Exercises

1. Write a list of self-criticisms/negative thoughts related to GOLF or BUSINESS or LIFE as it relates to you. Be 100% honest with yourself.

2. Address each criticism one-at-a-time.

3. DELETE the statement; discard it, because it no longer has any power over you.

4. For each Self Criticism/Negative thought, INSERT a replacement positive statement that will become your reality, your focus, and your new affirmation. (Refer to page 53 for affirmation definition.)

Examples:

1. GOLF: Oh, NO, not the water hole, (I will get out an old ball). Delete that thought. Insert: "The water is not my target. I will focus on the green".

2. Business: Nothing is going right for me at work right now. Delete that thought. Insert: "I am going to make some changes at work. I love my work and things get done with ease".

3. Life: I'm in a bad job, bad relationship and have an unhealthy lifestyle. I hate my life! Delete those thoughts. Think: "What can I change? "I love life and deserve to be happy."

Practice – Changing your thinking

Practice – Belief

Practice – Trust

NOTE: This takes practice, perseverance, belief, more practice, trust, desire and more practice.

1) _____

_____

_____

2) _____

_____

_____

3) _____

_____

_____

"I am enough."

"I deserve the best in life."

"I am loved."

Self Belief

The way we feel about ourselves, our work, our relationships and our ability to succeed whether it be in sport or other aspects of life, can be influenced by:

- o Negative words that have been spoken to or about us
- o Other people's opinions
- o Lack of love
- o Having been subjected to abuse
- o Lack of encouragement or support

These are all factors that contribute to low levels of self-esteem, self-love and self- respect.

Hopefully this book has given you an awareness, and instilled confidence and trust that **you can control your thoughts** and not be affected by negative influences. If you practice and put into play the techniques I have shared, you will have a much better chance of finding success and happiness on and off the golf course.

Examples of people who were knocked back or abused or told they were not good enough, but did not allow the negativity to hold them back from achieving their "intentional success" include:

Colonel Sanders	JK Rowling
Albert Einstein	Charles Darwin
Michael Jordan	Meryl Streep
Lady Gaga	Oprah Winfrey
Walt Disney	Elvis Presley
Marilyn Monroe	Stephen King
Thomas Edison	Dr. Seuss

Jenny Sevil

and soon to be . . . . .

Dreams

Really

Do

Come True

My Family

What's Your Driving Force?

DOWNLOAD YOUR
FREE BONUSES
AT

jennysevilthemindgame.com.au/bonuses

Made in the USA
Middletown, DE
04 March 2021